Taking a Risk

By **Raymond Gene Rojas**

Copyright © 2021 Raymond Gene Rojas

All rights reserved.

ISBN:987-0-578-24255-2

This book is dedicated to my mother Sylvia Rojas who took a Risk on myself, my twin brother, and my little sister. If it wasn't for you, I wouldn't be the man I am today. You have demonstrated unconditional love many times even when I didn't deserve it. You are and always have been my biggest supporter. I love you with all my heart. This one's for us #RojasStrong

FOREWARD

READ THIS BOOK AT YOUR OWN RISK!

As a passionate student of leadership I can attest to the fact that there is not one person who has had a great impact in culture who is not a risk taker. Risk-taking is a foundational discipline for those who aspire to change the world. In fact, I would say that without taking risks we rob the next generation from a brighter, better future; For when we risk nothing in the present, we risk everything in the future.

I have known Ray for a long time! More than just an incredible leader, pastor, and now author, Ray has always been a friend to me and my destiny. His commitment to his family and to his community have driven him to continue to take risks and to become the leader he is today. What I love about Ray is that his commitment to helping people is not reserved for those who attend his weekly gatherings, but now through this book we all get to read the stories and learn the lessons of a risk taker who models this message.

This book will inspire you to dream bigger, to find that God-given call that is within you. And more importantly, it will challenge you to take that risk that you have been putting off for a while. As you read through these chapters and become more aware of our generation's need for more risk takers, my prayer is that you will answer the call of God on your life to launch into the deep and lead with passion into a lifestyle of risk.

This world needs more risk takers! This world needs you! Like I said at the beginning of this foreword: Read this book at your own risk! Because once you see the greatness within you, you will not be able to unsee it. Let's all lean in, dream big and TAKE A RISK!

Your Friend,
Abe Camacho
Lead Pastor at Local Church San Diego
@abecamacho

Scripture quotations markerd (NLT) are taken from the Holy Bible, New Living Translation, copyright ©1996, 2004, 2007, 2013, 2015 by Tyndale House Foundation. Used by permission of Tyndale House Publishers, Inc., Carol Stream, Illinois 60188. All rights reserved.

Scripture quotations markerd (KJV) are from the King James Version of the bible

Scripture quotations markerd (NIV) are taken from the NEW INTERNATIONAL VERSION (NIV): Scripture taken from THE HOLY BIBLE, NEW INTERNATIONAL VERSION ®. Copyright© 1973, 1978, 1984, 2011 by Biblical, Inc.TM. Used by permission of Zondervan

Scripture quotations markerd (NKJV) are taken from the NEW KING JAMES VERSION (NKJV): Scripture taken from the NEW KING JAMES VERSION®. Copyright© 1982 by Thomas Nelson, Inc. Used by permission. All rights reserved.

Scripture quotations markerd (CSB) are taken from The Christian Standard Bible. Copyright © 2017 by Holman Bible Publishers. Used by permission. Christian Standard Bible®, and CSB® are federally registered trademarks of Holman Bible Publishers, all rights reserved.

Scripture quotations markerd (ASV) are taken from
NEW AMERICAN STANDARD BIBLE®,
Copyright © 1960,1962,1963,1968,1971,1972,1973,1975,1977,1995 by The Lockman Foundation. Used by permission."

TABLE OF CONTENTS

ACKNOWLEDGMENTS

Thank You Jesus for giving me the opportunity to speak from my heart.

To my beautiful SEXY Latina wife Cassandra.
I love you with all my heart and thank you for always being my biggest fan in life and throughout this journey. I can't see myself doing life with anyone else. Thank you for putting up with my dramatic self and all my crazy ideas. There is no me without you.

To my Church Fam,
Real Life Church San Diego is and will always be Family. I get to Pastor the greatest group of people in the whole world. We are definitely BETTER TOGETHER. I pray God continues to open doors and our best days are still ahead of us.

To my brothers from another mother
Josh Pascua, the moment we met it was game over. I've became a better man because of you. I love you brother. We are family, and nothing will ever change that. The calling on your life is remarkable. Sammy Famoso, there is no doubt your life is special and your calling is unique. Your gift in music and building relationships is something to cherish just like our friendship. Love you so much!

To my twin brother Rudy,
Man thank you for always being a brother. The world didn't deserve just one of us it needed both of us. Being a twin growing up it was "Rudy and Raymond" and I'm glad it's still being said. There is something special about you and I'm glad it's not hidden.

To my little sister Reyna,
You are one of a kind and there is no one like you. The world needs you more than you know. Our conversations are special, our snooping and our detective work on social media is shockingly impressive. I love you and thank you for making me a better human.

To my other siblings Jesse, Gene, Sylvia, and Savannah,
I love every single one of you. We carry the same blood because of dad, and I know dad would be proud of every single one of you. We are family forever.

To my children, Raymond, Noah, and Leia,
Daddy loves you all with all my heart. Everything I do is for you. Thank you for being Life to those around you and for making life so precious. The future is bright because of you three.

Tia Penny, Our Family is held together because of you and your faith. You are my second mother and I love you more than you'll ever know.

To my whole Rojas family, I Love you. #RojasStrong #MissAndLoveYouDadRIP

To everyone who is about to read this book, I pray it helps you see life differently and pushes you closer to your dreams. It all starts with a Risk.

Chapter 1
A Risk Taker

"Only those who will risk going too far can possibly find out how far it is possible to go." -T.S. Eliot

I think it's natural to want more in life. To be able to see farther than what's in front of you and not stop until it becomes a reality. Whether it's having more money, more success, more joy, or even more meaning to life. It's living a life beyond average. I knew life had more to offer than it was presenting, like going to IN N OUT and ordering animal style fries from the secret menu. There is always more. In 2013, Times 100 released its list of the 100 most influential people in the world full of celebrities from sports, film, drama, business, etc. During the interviews, a question was asked to all the nominated people, "What's the riskiest career decision you've ever made"? Bryan Cranston, known for his iconic role in Breaking bad as Walter White said

"The riskiest career decision is to go into this acting career. You have to be a risk-taker of some degree to be able to say, 'Alright, I'm throwing it all out there. Whatever happens, happens. I want to be an actor, even if it means sleeping on someone's couch for the rest of my life."

I don't think I know a lot of people who are willing to take a risk without a safety net underneath. Sleeping on a couch sounds tough and pretty hipster, but no one wants that journey. Nobody wants to take a risk but the decision of taking a risk must be made. Risk takers are fueled by courage. The dreams we hold in our hearts that are too embarrassed to share, say out loud, or too afraid to start, must change and begin within ourselves. If we change the way we think and begin with a mentality of "Alright, I'm throwing it all out there. Whatever happens, happens." You are taking the risk to step out into the unknown. Once we do, the risk is completed with a can-do mentality. This book began as notes, I would write to myself during seasons of taking risk. In this book I want to encourage you to see what happens when we take risk and look at life not through lens of fear but through lens of courage.

Risk takers are fueled by Courage

Becoming a risk taker requires courage like a vehicle requires gas to operate. but many times, courage is often replaced by negative energy we give to ourselves.

The possibility of what could go wrong before we even start thinking of the steps to take.

Our minds focus on the negative and what could go wrong like being stuck in a "What If" bubble, we avoid taking risks because these "what ifs" take root in our minds and start overshadowing our inner will and confidence. We were never called to live a "What If" life. What are the "What If's" in your life? What are the what ifs that held you back from advancing to the best you? See, a risk taker is not moved by how they succeed or fail, but on the solid foundation of not being trapped in the "What If" box. I would rather fail and know I at least tried than to go through life with a what if because I was too afraid of taking a risk.

We were never called to live a "what if" life

Risky decisions

We make decisions that are risky all the time. It's a risk to start a new job, or to move to a new city. We take a risk when we begin to date. Are they the right one? Will I get hurt? It's a risk to get married and be completely open to one another. The risk my wife took when she said "I do" would have to be the best decision she could have ever made. That's just my personal opinion. In life we make choices where the risk has little impact such as the outfit you wear, if you skip breakfast, or picking dinner reservations. It's the big risk with the big consequences we tend to avoid. Faith is something I've had ever since I was a kid, my mother would take my twin brother, my sister, and I to church. I believe we need faith to make any risk worth taking. Faith is knowing who is with you during the risk. We see many risks being taken in the bible and every time God was there.

The faith that motivated Abraham to go to a distant land at the age of 75. First of all, he was wealthy beyond measures, there was no need to leave where he was at and second of all THE MAN WAS 75! But he heard a word from

God and took the risk to trust God and went for it (Genesis 12). Sometimes all we need is just a word from God. That word is a covering over your calling in life which allows risk in your journey seem not to bad because you know who's with you.

Think about Peter for a moment, Matthew 14 tells the story about the risk Peter took. Scripture tells us that the disciples were in trouble. The disciples were on a boat and the wind was strong and the sea state was bad. Jesus came walking on water. In their fear the disciples thought it was a ghost (verse 26) but Jesus told them, "Don't be afraid," he said. "Take courage. I am here!"

"Then Peter called to him, "Lord, if it's really you, tell me to come to you, walking on the water." "Yes, come," Jesus said. So, Peter went over the side of the boat and walked on the water toward Jesus."

Matthew 14:28-29 (NLT)

During the storm Peter took a risk that has never been done before. Believing Jesus was with him, he did what no man before him and even after him have ever done. Peter got out of the boat and walked on water and walked towards Jesus.

This was definitely a risk people would have told you it was impossible to do. People would have told Peter no one can or ever will walk on water, it can't be done! The first step in a risk, is that the risk needs to be carried by faith, Peter took the first step through faith and walked on water. A risk taker will see what others cannot see. There is always going to be a what if staying in the boat is safer than the risk of drowning. Staying in the boat is where we feel safe. Its where we find comfort. Stepping out of the boat is discomfort, but in the discomfort, confidence is form. Your courage is altered. I can look back at how many times I stayed in the boat in my personal life. How many missed opportunities I had all because I didn't take a step of faith? One risk can have impact on your future.

Taking a risk is an investment in yourself. The more we start becoming a risk taker, the more we start prospering no matter what the condition is. As we go through these chapters, I really want to encourage you stop thinking of the outcomes, I want everyone to step out of the what if mentality, I want everyone to see their life from the lens of YES I CAN instead of the fear of failure.

Against all odds

There is a plethora of examples everywhere around us, Jeff Bezos the founder and owner of Amazon, started amazon as a bookstore in his garage in 1994 and today is the wealthiest person alive. Bezos is best known around the world for taking the boldest of the risks, in 2005 when he started amazon prime, he had a lot of critics saying that no one would be willing to pay $79 for his service and today the service has more than 100 million users including my wife and children . He believes that

"If you come up with a business idea and there's no risk there... It's probably already being done and done well. So, you have to have something that might not work, and you have to accept that your business in many ways is an experiment, and it might fail and that it's okay."

Bezos is just not the only person that took a risk against all odds, Elon Musk when he co-founded PayPal, no one believed that such a payment service would be even reliable, but we all know where that company went. But during its peak days, Elon sold 11.7% of his sales share to form Tesla and Space X, one company that he planned to go against the biggest space entity in the world NASA and the other company that he believed would develop Electric cars to shape the Future. Everyone ridiculed his idea of making Tesla, an electronic vehicle company because people believed that no one could step up into the world of the automobile giants and that too in the clique of Electronic vehicles that even names like Mercedes and BMW were afraid to go for. But Elon was persistent about his idea and took the risk, but at one point it seemed like it will all go in vain as both the companies were near bankruptcy, at this point Elon took the other risk and put everything he had in it and changed the outcome of his risk to success. Taking risks is what Musk does, and that has overcome all his failure, as he said in an interview

"I would encourage you to take risks now, to do something bold, you won't regret it."

Oprah Winfrey is known as the lady who appeared out of nowhere and became America's icon. Before her success, she was working as a co-anchor and was fired from the job because in their words: "she was unfit for television." She could have given up and accepted what they told her or continued on taking risks for a dream that was inside her to be on television. No one thought that the girl from Tennessee University, a girl no one knew about would end up becoming one of the most famous personalities of the nation. She took a risk by putting everything she had on the line. She was overlooked, full of self-doubt, all she needed was a moment, one moment to take a risk to change her life. She mentions that she was always going around asking directors for the films and kept getting rejected. Her lawyer said one thing to her that changed her.

"Well, you have to believe that you are worth the risk. If it doesn't work, you lose, but if you actually, really believe that it's going to work, you win big".

Are we risk takers?

All these people are the first names that come to mind who were risk takers despite what everything looked like and what everyone was saying. Risk takers adopt the traits of courage, of will power, of decision making and just let it all out and go into the world with the mentality of risking it all. We have the potential in us to be who we were called to be. Our full potential is found in our courage to risk take. All it demands from us is to get over our fear of risking and go with the flow of life.

We have the potential in us to be who we were called to be

Chapter 2

Becoming A Dream Chaser

"There is nothing like a dream to create the future."
– Victor Hugo

We need more dreamers in today's culture. There is a difference between a daydreamer and a dream chaser. Who is willing to step out of the box of normality? A dream chaser is people who won't settle for the average, people who are willing to chase their dreams to know there is more. It's effortless to dream. To be honest, it's really fun to dream. But the idea of chasing the dream and turning it into reality isn't fun. The idea of chasing anything already sounds exhausting. To come true for a dream, we need to risk our regular and step out, stretch, and begin to chase the dream. This is where it becomes a game-changer. Harriet Tubman once said, "Every great Dream begins with a dreamer. Always remember, you have within you the strength, the patience, and the passion to reach for the stars to change the world."

There is a difference between a Daydreamer and a Dream Chaser

Follow through

One thing I've struggled with is following through. I've quit more times than I've started. All because I thought I was dreaming the impossible. I allowed myself to believe the impossible isn't for me. I mean, who am I? Definitely not a Kardashian. So how can someone like me accomplish the impossible in my life? This makes me think of the story in Mark 5. The story begins in verse 25. It tells us a certain woman, which had an issue of blood for twelve years (KJV). First off, we do not even get her name. She is presented by her issue. Because of her issue, she was not allowed to be around or touch anyone. She was considered unclean. She gave her life savings to get better, and instead of getting better, she got worst. Her situation to get better looked impossible. When your situation looks impossible, you will start dreaming about the impossible. She was not going to give up despite what her situation looked like. Verse 27 tells us she heard of a man named Jesus, healing the blind, the sick, and the deaf. How faith of a mustard seed can heal the impossible, and she had dramatic faith. She had crazy faith; because of that, she did the un normal. She showed up where Jesus was. I keep thinking what the crowd was wondering in their heads like why is she here? But she was determined to do the impossible. Her faith had her saying

"if I can just put my finger on his garment, I'll get healed."

Her dream of being healed gave her good old fashion dramatic faith. Leading up to this, the stories she's been hearing were

Jesus touched and healed,

Jesus touched and healed,

Jesus touched, spit, touched again, and healed.

But she never heard a story of people saying they touched him and was healed, but her faith made her believe such a thing is possible. It was a risk of faith. Everyone was there for the same reason; picture this with me. She was in the middle of a crowd who came looking for hope. What made this woman who was known by her issue different from the rest was the fact she was tired of sitting in her situation and waiting for it to change on her own. Everybody wanted Jesus to touch them, she went to touch Jesus. She wanted her dream to be a reality. For your dream to become real, you need to take a risk and chase after it despite what everyone around you will think or say. Imagine if she never went to go see Jesus. Her desire to be healed would be a wishful dream.

I think of the late Nipsey Hussle; aside from having phenomenal music, Nipsey was also an entrepreneur. Nipsey referred to his dream as a marathon. In business and music. Nipsey explained the meaning of his brand Marathon in an interview he did with Big Boy on Big Boy's Neighborhood:

"That's why I call my thing a marathon. I'm not going to lie and portray this ultimate poise like I been had it figured out. Nah, I just didn't quit. That's the only distinguishing quality from me and probably whoever else going through this, went through this, or going through this is that I ain't quit. I went through every emotion to pursue what I'm doing."

When chasing your dream, you are in no competition with anyone else. It's a dream placed in your heart, no one else's, so chase it. If your dream is starting a business, moving to a new city, starting a new job, writing a book, creating a YouTube channel, or becoming a better person. The opportunity is yours if you dare enough to chase after it. There is no perfect time but the time you are in now. Do not limit your belief system because you are not living your dream.

Achieving your dreams comes with a lot of hard work, dedication, and a lot of risks.

I want the mentality of one who is willing to fight for my current outlook to match my dreams. Our dreams need to be big, and honestly, it needs to be scary that I won't accomplish by myself. These are dreams that require God to step in. If your dreams don't require God to step in, you're not dreaming big enough.

Don't limit your possibilities with God.

Dreamers

All great dreamers have a habit that makes them great achievers. They can see it. I love being around dreamers. They can see it before it's actually there. Great free-throw shooters in the NBA picture the ball going through the basket. PGA golfers picture the ball going straight down the fairway. This grooms the mind to control the body to carry out the dream. A dreamer sees what others can't. The difference between a dreamer and a day dreamer is the dreamer will make it a reality to pursue a new dream while the day dreamer stays on the same dream. Dreamers build success. They set goals along the way. It is one thing to set a goal and it's another thing to achieve that goal. Almost everyone sets goals but only a few possess the discipline to follow through on those goals. Dreamers acknowledge the risk they need to take in order to follow through. For example; I love spending time with church planters. These are my people. I love to hear where they see the church going, and what it's going to take to achieve it. The start to becoming a dream chaser begins with practicing what it means to break out of your comfort zone and seeing you have what it takes. Identify that you are a dreamer.

Inspired

One of the great things I love in life are movies. You name it, I've seen it. My kids were stuck on a particular movie for a while and I don't blame them, it is an incredible film. The movie is called Sing. Mathew McConaughey who voices Buster Moon, a koala who is unsuccessful, but still a dreamer. Moon decides to give his run-down theater a boost by staging a talent contest in hopes on saving his theater. What I love about this movie is everything points to failure from the beginning for Moon and yet Moon says this one incredible line while trying to help an elephant named Meena overcome her fear of singing in public that stuck with me: "Don't let fear stop you on doing what you love". Although it's just a movie, they do a really well job showing how not giving up no matter how many roadblocks you occur, how many failed attempts you've already had, and how many people will tell you it will not work. when it's just you and this dream, we need to hold on tight. We all have things we love to do in life, but sometimes we let fear get in our way of actually doing them. We are afraid of messing up, or afraid of being embarrassed in front of others, or afraid of failing…so instead we don't do that thing we love but Buster

Moon is a perfect example of a risk taker and a dream chaser and how the two goes hand in hand. Chase dreams with hope as each animal did once they arrived under Moon believing that this is their shot to change the course of their life. Hold on to your motive for chasing your dreams. You will never know what chasing your dream feels like unless you put your shoes on and begin to start chasing them. Start visualizing ahead of time what the end of the finish line looks like and manifest the outcome!

Success isn't always about greatness. It's about consistency. Consistent hard work leads to success. Greatness will come. - Dwayne "The Rock" Johnson

Keep dreaming

When you chase a dream more significant than you, it becomes a Risk. Risk of your dream being shattered. The antinode for shatter dreams is to dream again. You are never too old or too young to start chasing dreams. I haven't stopped. I'm still chasing dreams. I remembered launching Real Life Church. This was not a dream I was able to accomplish on my own. I knew I needed the right people to chase this dream with me.

What dream are you chasing? What risk are you willing to take to see that dream become a reality? If you dream of becoming famous, or becoming successful, wealthy, an influencer, what are the steps you are taking? The bigger the dream, the bigger the risk.

If your dreams don't require God to step in, you're not dreaming big enough

Chapter 3
Overcoming Fear
(Faith over Fear)

"Do one thing every day that scares you."

-Eleanor Roosevelt

I graduated high school over a decade ago. In 2016 I was contemplating if I was going to go back and receive my bachelor's degree. During my thought process, fear told me I was too old, that ship had sailed. I have too much on my plate. It'll never work. It took me three years to finally overcome the fear and make the decision to go back. It was the littlest fear I held on to that grew big inside of me. Going back to school was going to benefit me in the future but yet the thought of not being able to learn at my age pondered in me. I know that sounds ridiculous but that's what fear does. I have had many things in life that fear held me back on, but I think about this one particular moment. It took three years to overcome the fear. I would have been more than halfway done. It's ironic the power we give fear.

Powerless fear

The power that fear has, I realized, came from myself. I gave it the power it never originally had. Too often in my life, I've allowed fear to intervene and take root where I should have allowed faith to do so. I've given up on dreams all because the risk scared me. We really never genuinely follow through, or we end up quitting halfway because we fear the end result won't end up the same way as we predict it but taking a risk requires action. What blocks our action is our fear. Like myself, we want God to let us do big things, accomplish a lot that requires minimal risk only because we are afraid of a risk that requires a cost. It's easy to talk about taking a risk, overcoming fear because talk is cheap. Fear allows us to give excuses, but actions allow us to conquer fear and accomplish our dreams. We need faith in areas we are afraid of. Faith allows us to go through a circumstance knowing yes, I may be afraid, but I know God will get me through it. If faith was easy, everyone would be faithful. But God doesn't call the qualified; he qualifies those who are called. We see this in the story of David.

> If faith was easy, everyone would be faithful

David's faith helped him defeat Goliath.

In 1st Samuel chapter 17, we see Israel was at war with the Philistines in Elah's Valley. Standing on opposite sides of a hill, the Israelites and the philistines agreed to send one warrior from each side to fight, and whoever won would win the war.

The Philistines sent a man named Goliath, a Philistine giant who was over nine feet tall. Covered in fear, the Israelites had no one to send. Goliath, day after day, would mock the Israelites and challenge them to fight, mocking their God and feeding into their fears for 40 days. The fear the Israelites had in Goliath gave no future for the Israelites. What made David different from the rest of the Israelites is that David overcame Goliath by putting his fear to the side and relying on God's strength. Relying on God's strength is being able to fully trust God when conquering fear. David took a risk when everyone else stood in fear of Goliath because David's passion for God was more significant than the fear in Goliath.

God doesn't call the qualified; he qualifies those who are called

Faith over fear

What are you passionate about? If you have a passion for dancing or your passion is found in art, follow through. Take a risk and do more. Test your limits. What do you see yourself doing, and what kind of fear are you allowing to interfere with your future? People are torn on how to feel. Faith over fear doesn't mean that you don't feel afraid, it means that you will not let your fear consume you or your actions. Don't allow the fear to be a giant in your life. Allow your faith to be a bigger giant in your life.

Actions louder than words

Not too long ago I was at the barbershop. As I was getting my haircut, I was listening to the barber right next to me talk to his client as he cut his hair. It was one of those conversations where you forget there are other people in the room and you turn your inside voice into your outside voice, yeah; that was him. He continued to talk about how a man made money on being a middle person in business transactions and how you get paid to make sure the transactions are completed. He went on to say the man made a sufficient amount of money and will teach others how to do the same through a seminar in which they would have to pay for. First thing that went through my mind was "Wolf of Wall Street" but I wanted to hear more; not on what the business was but on how excited this barber was about this new life changing method. Two weeks later, I ended up back for my usual haircut and come to find out he was talking to another client of his, and the client was asking him if he ended up going to the seminar. The barber answered no and began to say the night before he began thinking that it was probably a scam and so on and so on. I was listening how he accused it not being real and how they just wanted his money, so he ended up sleeping in that morning and playing call of duty the whole day. This has become normal. Words with no meaning. Emotions with no action. Whether it was a scam or not and to be honest I don't really care, what got to me was him not taking the risk to find out. Let's say it was not real, that conversation would have been different. Talk is cheap. This is what separates good from great. When you think of inspiring leaders, or successful role models we can see the common characteristics they share and that's delivering their promised result. They inspire by doing, not talking. As a pastor, demonstrating God's love by my actions towards people makes a bigger impact than just saying God loves you. I want my actions to identify where I'm going and not have fear dictate why I should stay. The problem with the barber is he allowed doubt to intervene which created fear of the unknown. Allow your actions to be moved by faith.

Liar liar PANTS ON FIRE

Have you ever noticed fear has a voice only because we allow it to speak to us?

Fear will always tell you the risk isn't worth the heartache. It isn't worth the embarrassment. "If you move forward and fail everyone will know it." Fear keeps you still, not allowing you to grow. A few years back, I said at a conference I was speaking at: "Fear keeps you comfortable in the uncomfortable." This is no way to live. What are you being called to do? What change do you have to make? What Goliath do you need to take head-on? Take the risk, be bigger than fear.

Fear keeps

you

comfortable

in the

uncomfortable

Here's what the scriptures say about fear:

+ Isaiah 41:10 (NIV) So do not fear, for I am with you; do not be dismayed, for I am your God. I will strengthen you and help you; I will uphold you with my righteous right hand.

+ Isaiah 41:13 (NIV) For I am the LORD, your God, who takes hold of your right hand and says to you, do not fear; I will help you.

+ Matthew 10:28 (NKJV) And do not fear those who kill the body but cannot kill the soul. But rather fear Him who is able to destroy both soul and body in hell.

+ 1 Corinthians 16:13 (CSB) Be alert, stand firm in the faith, be courageous, be strong.

+ Hebrews 13:5-6 (NKJV) For He himself has said, "I will never leave you nor forsake you." So we may boldly say: "The LORD is my helper; I will not fear. What can man do to me?"

+ Deuteronomy 31:6 (NKJV) Be strong and of good courage, do not fear nor be afraid of them; for the LORD your God, He is the One who goes with you. He will not leave you nor forsake you.

+ Psalm 27:1 (NLT) The LORD is my light and my salvation— so why should I be afraid? The LORD is my fortress, protecting me from danger, so why should I tremble?

+ 2 Timothy 1:7 (ASV) For God gave us not a spirit of fearfulness; but of power and love and discipline.

+ 1 John 4:18 (NIV) There is no fear in love. But perfect love drives out fear because fear has to do with punishment. The One who fears is not made perfect in love.

+ 1 Chronicles 28:20 (NIV) David also said to Solomon, his son, "Be strong and courageous and do the work. Do not be afraid or discouraged, for the LORD God, my God is with you. He will not fail you or forsake you until all the work for the service of the temple of the LORD is finished.

To Summarize:

Fear can lead us to overthink a decision, factoring in variables you have no way to predict. This can lead to analysis paralysis and often crazy decisions.

Fear can cause us to put off or avoid some decisions, which often results in lost options and worse decisions, not better.

Fear can reduce the number of decisions you make so that, over time, your decision-making abilities do not improve. Every decision is unnecessarily rigid and often comes with poor results.

So, it's time you put on the face of courage and step over fear!

Chapter 4
The Risk of Failing

"When you take risks, you learn that there will be times when you succeed, and there will be times when you fail, and both are equally important." - Ellen DeGeneres

If I were to list a list of things I'm good at, I would write down I'm good at eating. There's no argument there. I love good food. I would also write down I'm good at talking to people. I am what you may call a social butterfly. I can talk and talk and talk. High key I'm good at memorizing every Drake lyric. I'm good at my work ethics. I'm good at making cute kids, HELLO! Come on somebody. But also, in this list of things I'm good at, if I'm honest with myself I would write that I, Raymond Rojas is good at failing. I have failed in many areas of my life. If I ever tried to begin a new project, past failures I've had will tell me, "why would I succeed this time?" I believe we have all failed at one point in our lives, if it was in a marriage, as a parent, in a brand-new business, or even as a friend. Let's face it; no one likes to fail. It hurts! It's embarrassing, and It's our pride that often takes the biggest hit. Failing is an experience no one wants to experience ever again. And if you're like me, we tend to avoid it at all costs instead of learning from it and trying again.

To fail, you've had to take a risk.

It's almost impossible to hear a story of success that didn't have a trail of mistakes behind it. How is that possible? We only see the results, but never the journey it took that had so many pit stops.

We look at successful icons such as Michael Jordan and think he was the lucky one born with such an incredible gift, not knowing the journey was long and hard. Michael Jordan once said in a Nike commercial, "I've missed more than 9,000 shots in my career. I've lost almost 300 games. 26 times, I've been trusted to take the game-winning shot and missed. I've failed over and over and over again in my life. And that is why I succeed." Today, Jordan is considered one of the greatest basketball players of all time (I'm more of a Kobe fan, but the respect is there). Nearly everyone has experienced failure at some point in their life. The key to overcoming obstacles and becoming successful starts with learning from your mistakes. I see this for our everyday lives. Becoming better than who we were yesterday is a journey to becoming the best version of you.

"My flesh and my heart may fail, but God is the strength of my heart and my portion forever."

Psalms 73:26 (NIV)

The key to overcoming obstacles and becoming successful starts with learning from your mistakes

It's how we look at failure.

Failure should not be looked at as an ending point. But as an opportunity to try again. New ideas are to explore many ways until the right one is the right one.

I improve as a person by not repeating the same mistakes I make. But finding new ways to improve.

Thomas A. Edison once stated:

"I have not failed. I've just found 10,000 ways that won't work."

One thing I always need to remind myself of is that failure isn't permanent. It may feel like it's permanent at the moment, it may look like it's permanent, but You were never called to live a life of failure. Failure is one thing everyone has in common. But only a few have taken a risk to try again. The goal is to be in the few. Just because you failed in a relationship, at work, in business, even in your walk with God does not mean you should bury all your aspirations and resign to the couch with ice cream and Netflix. It just means that on this occasion, whatever actions you took did not generate the results you wanted. Lean on the areas that did not work to improve. Our perception of failure needs to change.

You were never called to live a life of failure.

In moments of weakness, don't destroy yourself.

We are not perfect, just willing to be perfected. Stop looking at failure as a bad thing and more a moment of opportunity. New beginnings. My best always comes right after a failed moment. It took a long time for this mentality. I used to tune life out and throw a pity party for me, myself, and I every time I encountered a failed moment. But your growth from failure measures your maturity for your success in your future.

Failure should not be looked at as an ending point. But as an opportunity to try again

The outside viewers

Another reason why we tend to avoid failure is because we worry too much of the outside perception. You know, the ones who are not involved and don't want to be involved but still have an input. Yes, them. The people who whisper your success but will shout your failures.

There are people we know who watch fail attempts and it validates how taking a risk isn't worth it, so when they see you taking a risk, they are quick to give their opinion on how much better it is staying safe in the confines of old choices. Sometimes we fail simply because we are too worried about what other people are thinking. Let's be real, people are entitled to think whatever they want, just as you are entitled to think what you want. So, if they disagree or have nothing but negativity; it's only outside views. Key word outside. You are doing what they choose to not do. Take risk, build your future, make new choices. What people think of you cannot change who you are or what you are worth, don't give outside viewers that power. This is your life to live. Live life to the fullest, believe beyond the risk into your future and at the end of the day you are the only person who needs to approve of your own choices. Remember that growth and learning take place when you're operating at the edge of your capacity. Take the risk, look beyond failure.

"Care about what other people think and you will always be their prisoner."

– Lao Tzu

Taking a risk makes you adapt to growth.

One of our favorite sayings in the church is, "we serve a God of second chances." If you are like me, I live off second chances. I live off the grace that the first time was not my last time. I was who Jesus was talking about when he told Peter to forgive 70 x 7 times in Matthew 18. Because every second chance is an opportunity for a new outcome. Failure creates new opportunities. Many people believe that everything happens for a reason; we just don't know what it is at the time. Failures often bring unforeseen opportunities that would not have been available without the failure in the first place. You often need to close one door so that another door of opportunity can be opened for you. Failure is a way of one door closing. Failure is seldom the end; it is often a bright beginning.

Your growth from failure measures your maturity for your success in your future.

Failure provides answers. If you don't try and fail, you will never know if your idea or method will work. You spend time worrying that you don't have the answer; you wonder whether it would have worked. The pain of regret is far worse than the pain of failure. When you fail, you can start again; with regret, you will never know.

Failure gives you the best chance of success. Research has shown that those who are at the top of their field are the ones who have failed the most.

Having to persevere to learn a new skill gives you the advantage over someone who gets it right the first time. Learning many ways how not to do it gives you the edge over the person who has not had that experience.

Failure is one thing everyone has in common. But only a few have taken a risk to try again.

Conclusion:

There cannot be a success without failure. As you pursue your dreams, you will come across failure. One saying goes, "failure doesn't stop people; it's how people handle failure that stops them." Remember When you encounter failure, will you take the opportunity to learn from your mistakes?

Every idea we have, or carry isn't going to work. It's

essential to take the time to organize your thoughts after a failure and realize what you did wrong and be willing to learn and grow. Anyone can succeed. It just comes down to how bad you want it!

Don't view failure as bad luck, instead look at each attempt to reach your goals as a triumph. There's always something to learn, ways to grow, different viewpoints to see, and new opportunities waiting just around the corner. So, get in and have a go. Fail fast and recover quickly to try again. Use every failure as an opportunity to learn and to grow as a person. Remember that every failure is like one step on the stairway to success. Above all else, remember this: If you never fail, you will never succeed.

Failure creates new opportunities

Chapter 5

A Self-Made Cheerleader

"The worst loneliness is to not be comfortable with yourself." -Mark Twain

In November 2018, Hollywood Boulevard was brought to a standstill as hundreds of fans flooded the streets to see one of his generation's most successful rappers, platinum-selling rap veteran Snoop Dogg to Receive his very own star on the Hollywood Walk of Fame. This was an iconic moment for fans and the hip-hop industry as icons like Dr. Dre, Quincy Jones, and Jimmy Kimmel spoke on Snoop's legacy. What made this a moment to look back on? During his acceptance speech, Snoop thanked his wife, his fans, Dr. Dre, his mother, and so many others for helping Snoop Dogg be Snoop Dogg. The last person he thanked that made headlines was HIMSELF.

"I want to thank me for believing in me, I want to thank me for doing all this hard work," he said. "I wanna thank me for having no days off. I wanna thank me for never quitting. I wanna thank me for always been a giver and trying to give more than I receive. I want to thank me for trying to do more right than wrong. I want to thank me for just being me at all times. Snoop Dogg, you a bad mother f*****."

It starts in your mind

Moments like this are essential. If you are not willing to celebrate or acknowledge yourself, you can't expect others to do the same thing. No one is going to celebrate you more than you. If you missed that, let me rephrase it. No one should celebrate you more than you. You need to Gas yourself up. The dreams you have, the ideas you carry, God wants you to flourish in it. But you can't advance if you can't believe in yourself. One of the healthiest things you can do for yourself is to speak life into yourself. To be a self-made cheerleader means you are setting yourself up to be mentally healthy.

Many psychology studies attest self-love and compassion is critical for mental health and well-being, keeping depression and anxiety at bay. The words that come out your mouth about yourself should be positive and life-changing.

"Don't use foul or abusive language. Let everything you say be good and helpful, so that your words will be an encouragement to those who hear them."

Ephesians 4:29 (NLT)

"Why is self-love important?" For many of us, self-love might sound like a luxury rather than a necessity — or a new-age fad for those with too much time on their hands.

Ironically, however, self-care and compassion might actually be needed most by those who work too hard and always strive to surpass ourselves and grasp the shape-shifting phantasm of perfection.

Most of the time, when we're too hard on ourselves, we either have a hard time believing we can achieve or we do it because we're driven by a desire to excel and do everything right, all the time. This entails many self-criticisms, and that persecutory inner voice that continually tells us how we could've done things better is a hallmark of perfectionism.

Studies have shown that perfectionists are at a higher risk of several illnesses, both physical and mental and that self-compassion might free us from its grip. Therefore, perfectionism and self-compassion are inextricably linked.

Speak life, not death

It's organic to celebrate yourself. Don't let anyone tell you differently. How can someone celebrate you if you can't celebrate yourself? I have three children; two boys and one girl. Ever since they were able to speak, I would ask each of them individually a list of questions each day: "who's amazing? Who's awesome? Who's handsome/beautiful? Who's going to grow up and do amazing things?" After each question, they would respond with "me." So, as they grow older, they have the mentality that they are amazing, unique, beautiful, and they will grow up and do amazing things. Loving yourself builds a healthy future. It builds self-confidence.

"for God gave us a spirit not of fear but of power and love and self-control."

2 Timothy 1:7 ESV

Loving yourself builds a healthy future. It builds self-confidence.

Self-Confidence vs. Self-Esteem

What happens when we hit a point where we are unable to celebrate ourselves? I've been in this position a lot of my adulthood.

I always felt like I was not good enough. Every mistake I made was personal to me as if I was not able to let it go. So, it became easier to celebrate others but not myself. This type of living was not healthy for my self-esteem. It doesn't build the confidence to take on life. Although self-confidence and self-esteem have crossed paths at many points and share some standard features, they are considered two distinct constructs.

Self-esteem is a reasonably stable trait that doesn't change much in individuals—unless they put in some dedicated effort to improve it. It can generally be defined as our beliefs in our own inherent value, worth, and how deserving we are of love, happiness, success, and other good things in life.

By contrast, self-confidence does not consider any beliefs about the worthiness or overall value; instead, it focuses on the ability to succeed and beliefs about one's likelihood of succeeding.

The two are positively related, but it is easy to see where the line is drawn between them; self-esteem is about the success you feel you deserve, while self-confidence is about the success you feel you can achieve

The Importance of Believing in Yourself

Not only does it simply feel right to believe in yourself, self-confidence and self-belief also brings about other desirable benefits.

It's Found in God

As a Christian, I define my self-esteem as having confidence that I am who God says I am. Knowing who God says I am will eliminate what other people say I am or say what I'm capable of doing. Self-support is fueled by God's words towards you.

"This is my command—be strong and courageous! Do not be afraid or discouraged. For the Lord, your God is with you wherever you go."

(Joshua 1:9 NLT)

When you don't feel like you're good enough, it's easy to tell ourselves to blend in, hide in the back, and avoid bringing any attention.

But God commands you to be healthy and courageous! The confidence is found not in your own abilities or strengths, but because God said he will be with you wherever you go. You can live in confidence because of his strength.

Our confidence becomes positive in our outlook on life. Our happiness is found in not others but in ourselves. When you are your biggest fan, other people's opinion of you will not affect you.

When we seek acknowledgment from others. It will keep you stuck.

Do not give in to negative self-talk and self-hatred. It's a road many people choose because they feel no other option.

Cling to God's truth and the healthy identity He's been restored in you. Take this as an opportunity that God has placed in you to dig a little deeper into whatever the more significant issue is. Spend some more time reflecting on a healthy identity to self-confidence.

Leading through risk

You have to enter any risk with the mentality that you can fulfill your dream. You have to believe in yourself to succeed. This is also important as being a leader.

The Importance of Self-Confidence in Leadership is paramount. I love the ideal thought of without confidence, there is no leadership. Leadership requires confident decision-making, bold but measured risk-taking, and commitment: three things that those with low self-confidence generally lack.

As Dao notes, self-confidence is also essential for employees to see in leaders; nothing boosts employees' belief in the organization and their own contributions than seeing the confidence and a similar belief in the organization's leadership.

In fact, self-confidence was identified as one of the defining characteristics of leaders in an influential early leadership study. Effective leadership requires at least a minimum level of self- confidence.

DJ KHALED

You are who you say you are. Your words have power. You can build yourself or destroy yourself. One thing I love about DJ Khaled is the life he speaks to others and especially towards himself. He is his number one fan. I learned from DJ Khaled the more you cheer for yourself, the more inner peace you receive. You build your own happiness from within you and not from what's around you. Khaled once said

"If you don't wake up in the morning, look in the mirror and say you're the greatest, and you the one then what are you?

Team captain

Who are you? I can tell you who you are not. You aren't a failed marriage. You are not failed entrepreneur. You are not a mistake to your parents. You are not the negative thoughts that are in your head. God has already said you are fearfully and wonderfully made, you are loved, valued, and the calling on your life is remarkable. Let's celebrate ourselves. You are exactly where you need to be at this very moment. Celebrate it. Even if you need to look in the mirror and remind yourself, your team captain of this cheerleading squad and you are going to shout yourself out.

Chapter 6
The Danger of the Comfort Zone

"If we're growing, we're always going to be out of our comfort zone." - John Maxwell

One thing I used to not like was change. The idea of Change was the worst. I think this came from lousy teaching. Just a bunch of lousy advice growing up. The "play it safe" route. The "don't get a credit card because you'll mess up your credit." "Just get any job to be stable." Play it safe. Playing it safe will get you by, but the only issue was I saw no future, and that scared me. I wanted more. If you were like me, I wanted the feeling of accomplishment to be fulfilled with little to no work being done. Instead of setting goals, I would daydream about finding a bag of money or having an inheritance given to me or winning the lotto. Surely this will help me reach the accomplishments I have in life in the comfort of my bed. I wanted success in my comfort zone. A comfort zone can be defined as a state of mind in which people are at ease, safe zones, stress-free zones where Timon and Pumbaa are teaching you "Hakuna Matata." Comfort zones are in control of their environment.

Therefore, the best way to define a comfort zone would be a state of mind where a person's anxiety and vulnerability are minimized to manageable levels. It is that area of your life in which you feel familiar with and in control of.

For example, some people love to go to work every morning and are used to the routine of working daily. Their work becomes their comfort zone, and leaving this comfort zone to become a freelancer or start a business can be challenging. Of course, for others, a comfort zone could be when they sit and eat while watching Vampire Dairies on Netflix or with social media after a hectic day. Of course, comfort zones are not static because they change based on your life's areas you feel most comfortable with.

When are you out of your comfort zone?

What is outside your comfort zone? What makes you begin to feel vulnerable, anxious, stressed? What makes you uncomfortable about doing something un-normal from your everyday life?

"A comfort zone is a beautiful place, but nothing grows there."

The Psychological States

According to White Alasdair, there are three psychological states: the comfort zone, optimal performance zone, and the danger zone. Where the comfort zone is the stress-free zone that you are familiar with. The optimal performance zone is the zone outside your comfort zone, where your performance is enhanced by some amount of stress. The danger zone, which is beyond the optimal performance zone, is where you feel high anxiety, and your performance is below the performance you can attain in your comfort zone.

However, the problem is making distinctions between these psychological states and knowing when and how far you are willing to leave your comfort zone and when to stay in its confines.

Why do you need to leave your comfort zone? Let's look at some reasons:

1. Stunted Growth

If you insist on staying in your comfort zone, you will probably never grow to be more than you are. That means you will always be stuck, never moving forward, and never growing. This was a regular part of my life. Most people who become addicted to their comfort zones usually end up unable to achieve their goals because they're somewhat obsessed with doing things the same way they've always done them even when it's not producing results. As a result, you can never really explore what you're capable of doing and what you can

accomplish if you stick to your comfort zone

2. To find your passion

Not moving out of your comfort zone makes it harder for you to discover your passion because no passion can ever be found in your comfort zone; it can only be found by stepping away from your comfort zone. Until then, it's just daydreaming.

3. To make sure you don't settle for less

Even though you've not found anything that makes your heartbeat very fast (like love or passion), your comfort zone might push you to settle for less than what you could have if you just stepped out of it.

Most people who become addicted to their comfort zones usually end up unable to achieve their goals because they're somewhat obsessed with doing things the same way they've always done them even when it's not producing results.

Discomfort

"To move to a new level in your life, you must break through your comfort zone and do things that are not comfortable."

– T. Harv Eker.

There are two things I'm not a fan of, they both bring me discomfort in life but yet benefit my life tremendously. The first one is dieting, and the second is stretching. I realized I needed both amid Covid-19. I was lying in the comfort of my home, in my room on my bed, the safest place I can be in the most comfortable way I can be; with no shirt wearing soccer shorts from 12 years ago, watching the most incredible saga God has ever blessed mankind with Star Wars when my daughter enters from the shadows of the four corners of the room jumps on my bed, rubs my belly and with the biggest smile on her face and says "Daddy your tummy is really big!" Now, this betrayal cuts deep because up to that point, she was my favorite one out of my three kids (I have no favorites, don't judge me), and at that moment, I realized she was right. I got comfortable with the gyms being closed; I was eating without a care in the world.

I mean, just the other day, my friend Wael and I both ate each a medium box of pizza in one sitting. A WHOLE BOX to myself. It was an incredible moment. Not so much afterwards as I complained to Wael on being in a food coma. So, it's safe to say she had a point. So instead of putting my daughter up for adoption or dropping her off at the fire station in a basket, I decided I needed to get out of my comfort zone and change my usual. So, there I go, I find my way to my old high school football field since the gyms are closed. I began to run, and less than 5 minutes, I am on the ground, ready to walk into the white light. I needed to stretch. My body was so tight and stretching only brought pain. It was in this discomfort I knew it will bring me growth. I knew the pain was only for now, and if I endure now, I will benefit from this in the long run. What I've come to learn is we stop when the comfort is no longer comfort. Safe zones are no longer safe. If I'm to take a risk in life, I want to cushion all around me but in discomfort, we find out what we are really made of. We find out who we are. We find out a lot about ourselves when we take risks. In our discomfort, we discover what makes us tick and begin to see that part of ourselves deep inside, our true self, then we can open doors to change, growth, progress, love, and understanding that cannot be found inside your comfort zone.

In discomfort, we find out what we are really made of

Life begins at the end of your comfort zone.

Experiencing life can never happen while being bound by chains. There is so much more for you. We were meant to live an abundant life (John 10:10 NKJV) in every area and season. We have to be committed to ourselves to take bold risks if we seek to become the best bold version of ourselves. Baby steps are essentials, especially when moving out of our comfort zone. Rome was not built in one day. It took me a week at the football field to run a mile without stopping. Every day I had to make an effort to stretch. And little by little, improvement came. It's little results that make a significant impact. Small steps confront your fears while managing discomfort. Personal growth becomes apparent beyond our comfort zone when extending ourselves. We celebrate our gains as we accomplish new levels each day and emotional strength and confidence along the way. When I worked in management at Panda Express, the one thing they always wanted for us was an improvement. Not just at work but also in life. We had to read and study, which became one of my favorite books by the late Stephen R. Covey: The 7 Habits of Highly Effective People. Covey reminds us, "It takes an enormous amount of internal security to begin with the spirit of adventure, the spirit of discovery, the spirit of creativity. Without doubt, you have to leave the comfort zone of base camp and confront an entirely new and unknown wilderness. You become a trailblazer, a pathfinder. You open new possibilities, new territories, new continents, so that others can follow."

It's little results that make a significant impact

I believe God moves outside of our comfort zone. I want God to do big things in my life. A good friend of mine who Pastors a phenomenal church in the heart of San Diego told me when we move, God moves. God moves off the faith of his people. Faith will change how we feel, how we see life, and how we build our future away from comfort and more towards faith in God. It takes us to be consistent, especially when we don't want to; this creates discipline. Which is the nail to the coffin towards the comfort zone?

If you've had an idea, dream, plan, or vision manifesting in your brain that you wanted to accomplish – why not use this year to make it happen? The hardest part is making the decision and committing to it. Following through and staying disciplined. Maybe it's moving across the country or finding another job… or even if it's starting a new exercise program or learning a new trade. If it's a fire in your heart, make the decision first to leave the comfort zone. Take the risk and know you are worth it. Tell people and just go for it. You'll realize that change isn't nearly as terrifying as the idea of leaving the comfort zone.

"It was character that got us out of bed, commitment that moved us into action, and discipline that enabled us to follow through."

- Zig Ziglar

Chapter 7
Finding Your Reason

"The most important thing is to try and inspire people to be great at whatever they want to do."

- Kobe Bryant

I once worked for a company called Gold Rush. My job titled was District Sales Leader. It was a fantastic job, and I was really good at it. I was the assistant to the district manager for all the San Diego locations, stretching out to Temecula. My duties vary from multiple roles from interacting with employees to interacting with customers to testing gold like a mad scientist. One thing I'd enjoy doing was training new employees for the company. New faces that are anxious to learn and dabble in the knowledge of gold, silver, and platinum.

During training, the company would want to focus on having the new employees understand how we do things.

I would explain there is a "why" in everything we do and explain what is the why. You couldn't live up to your full potential if you didn't know the why. It is an essential. It helps to give an understanding of the process. This was the reason the company existed. I think about the risk we take in life and why we take them. The "whys" in our life. There's always a why behind the attempt that has the potential to change and impact our lives. In my thirties, I've realized my why is so much different from my why in my twenties. I've learned there's a why behind everything we do. And I don't just want any why to be my reason. I want my why to challenge my future. Ask yourself, what is your why to your dreams? What is your reason behind every move you make?

Why do you go to work every day? Why do we set the alarm at night? Why do we wait for the very last minute to fill up gas in the car? Why are we reading this book? Why did we choose to eat pizza instead of a salad? Why do we choose to daydream instead of taking the risk? I believe it's because we haven't found our reason. The why is there but no reason behind it? We ignore the risk because the reason to take the risk does not seem too important to jeopardize the comfort you are in. I remind myself of my why several times a day because it keeps me focused mentally and excited about my goals.

Why's are personal. They remind you of what matters to you. Your reasons for doing something won't ever be precisely the same as anyone else's. They just need to inspire you.

We ignore the risk because the reason to take the risk does not seem too important to jeopardize the comfort you are in.

What motivates you

Your why should be very important to your risk and your everyday life. What pushes you to be the best you can be and not keep you stuck in the same place as you were last year. My reason to do better and be better and to take more risks are the people I go home to every day. For my wife and my three children. They make me want to be a better person, a better father, a better husband, Pastor, son, brother, and friend. My wife is incredible. (no, she's not the one writing this part. It's all me.) I don't believe I would be the man I am without her. Cassandra and I have been dating since high school. I first met Cassandra when she and her friends wanted to ditch school to go eat outside of school because Cassandra just got her first car and she was the only one in her friends who had a car at the time. A 2004 Ford Taurus. (I miss that car.)

Feeling almighty and powerful because of the car, she was the only one who could not leave school because she had no pass from her friends. Jumping the fence and running to the parking lot was not a risk she was willing to take. They told her to "go talk to a guy named Ray, he will help you to get out." First of all, what a burn! Did I help her ditch and be truant? I did and the result led to marriage with three little humans who call me dad and ask for Fortnite V-Bucks. Years later and memories build, she is still my reason to be better and to do better. She encourages me when I'm discouraged. She speaks life when my spirit is dead.

To find your reason to take a risk, you need to know what is motivating you. Is it as healthy as you think it is? I was reading the book Mamba Mentality by the Mamba himself, Kobe Bryant. In the book, Kobe talked about his love for the sport. He wanted to win; he wanted to be the best. So, he started to surround his life around winning. He was disciplined in every area. In the gym, in his diet, in his therapy in recovery, and what he read. His motivation to be the best transformed his life to become the best. Your motivation will help clarify and set up your goal. When you're motivated, you have a desire to create momentum to change your life. That's the goal, right? To be better than we were yesterday. Goals are the steppingstones toward your dreams, so to take a risk and achieve them, you need the momentum to keep you pushing forward towards them.

Your why is your best inspiration.

What are you fighting for?

When taking a risk, some have been more successful than others. That does not mean to give up. It just means you have to fight harder. A new approach is a new risk. Take more chances for yourself. Taking chances on yourself will help you accept that you can make the right choices and cope with the bad ones. Like we said earlier in the book, every successful person has first experience failure. It looks different for everyone, but what makes you stand out from others around you is the thrive to not quit and the pursuit to keep fighting for your dreams until they become a reality. A constant reminder to yourself that risks are almost always necessary for innovation and for progress. Who you are today are the results of the risk you have taken, or because of the risk you didn't take? The will to fight or not having the will to fight.

A new approach is a new risk

"But as for you, be strong and courageous, for your work will be rewarded.""

2 Chronicles 15:7 (NLT)

We all have big dreams and big goals. Every day needs to be a constant battle. It's not all glitter and gold. Life is unpredictable, and it's how we choose to act on our most challenging, most difficult days that make us who we are. I want to fight to make every risk I take to succeed because my reason outweighs the fear of staying behind. Your reason to take risks and be better will have you fight to be the person you need to be. In the most challenging times, during your darkest moments, when you feel like throwing in the towel, remind yourself why you are doing this. Why you are fighting. Your reason will always carry more value than giving up.

My reasons for taking the risk I take to improve and succeed are better than the reasons I have to quit. Especially when I know God is with me every step of the way.

I want to fight to make every risk I take to succeed because my reason outweighs the fear of staying behind.

Hold on to the reason.

Everybody's reason is different. What inspired you might not inspire the person next to you. That's okay. Your reason might be to be the first in your family to graduate college, or it might be to be financially stable or to be your own boss, or it might even just want to be a better person. This is your reason. Your reason has to be personal. Nothing will make a person get out of daydreaming and more into a dream chaser than their reason. Our reason at Real Life Church is to point people to Jesus. People from all walks of life can walk through our doors and experience a relationship with Jesus. Where you can find grace, hope, acceptance, restoration, and truth. You don't have to believe to belong because God already accepted you. This was my why when launching the church. A place where you can belong. At Real Life Church we want the community, the people, and our city to be impacted with God's love. We encounter Gods love through engaging worship, ministry, and biblical teaching. Spreading God's love is only the beginning. No background will ever disqualify you from a relationship with Jesus. My momentum is people. Knowing your why keeps you focused. Your momentum will make you take the risk. Why's give you that push you need to get started and help keep you focused as you're working toward your goal. Whys give you hope. They give you something to look forward to. Keeping the end result in mind.

Nothing will make a person get out of daydreaming and more into a dream chaser than their reason

Chapter 8
Growing Pains

"The tiny seed knew that in order to grow, it needed to be dropped in dirt, covered with darkness, and struggle to reach the light." -Sandra Kring.

Growth is so essential to life. We should be growing every day, spiritually, physically, and mentally. And not just with age. Self-growth is a lifelong process; from the moment of birth to our last breath on earth, it is something that happens every day even though you may not notice it at the moment. I desire to grow as an individual; I believe my talent can be developed (through hard work, right strategies, and wise counsel.) This is having a growth mindset. A growth mindset thrives on challenges and sees failure "not as evidence of unintelligence but as a heartening springboard for growth and for stretching our existing abilities." We should be living to grow, but we stop in the middle of the process many times. We feel stuck in a rut – like we are merely existing rather than actually living. We see other people living their best lives on social media and wish we could live a life of greatness, but greatness can't happen in yesterday's same environment. These are when we need to be willing to embrace change, take ownership, and realize that our growth and happiness ultimately depend on us alone. Yesterday is done and today is new. Each day is new. Every day is a new day, a new day of opportunity, the opportunity to change. Each day is a gift, and every day is unique, so do not worry about yesterday's flaws. One of my role models in life who made a big impact on my perspective, which is a five-time world champion and arguably one of the best NBA players to ever don a basketball jersey, the Black Mamba Kobe Bryant. He was a particular type of breed.

Kobe said in an interview he doesn't believe in failure. Ironic, right?! "Failure doesn't exist." Bryant's comments about failure are fascinating and mind-opening. His perceptions of failure are based on the fact that "the story continues." If you fail on Monday, you have Tuesday to try again. Bryant explains that the only way to fail is to "stop and to not learn." So, if you learned from the failure and went on to grow and improve your game, it wasn't a failure. The same words applied to the court can be applied in our lives. We have the power to flip the script. We can measure our success by how much we grow and learn, not by the outcome. Be the best that YOU can be and not measure our success against other people's success.

We should focus on one thing: Forgetting the past and looking forward to what lies ahead."
(Philippians 3:13 NLT)

I can look back in life where I've felt I've failed and other areas I've experienced the pain of a lot of my poor choices. Carrying the mamba mentality like Kobe was not a mindset I had at the time, so instead, I'd entertain the thought that I have blown it, I've failed, that God can't use a person like me, and there's no hope for restoration. This feeling is comfort, and more than anything, it's Familiar. I don't think I'm alone. I think we all face these feelings when we fail. When we take a risk, and it does not go the way we wanted it to. During these times, I draw strength from God's word.

The Bible is full of stories of heroes of the faith, followers of Jesus, who have blown it. Made mistakes like you and I. Their failures are so extreme; our natural thought is God would have turned His back on them. But this isn't God's personality. God is all about redemption. God is all about new days with a new opportunity. So when we feel like we've failed, we can be thankful that God gives us the new opportunity on a new day to do better to change our life and to grow into a better you. God loves a comeback story. Paul tells us in the bible that

"in all things God works for the good of those who love him, who have been called according to His purpose." (Romans 8:28 NIV)

This gives hope. This tells us no matter what happened today or yesterday, our adventure isn't over. Our journey continues. God's at work reclaiming our story.

We all have the opportunity to grow into the new you. To take a new risk and say I'm done with the way I'm living, I want change. You can't change unless you want to. You may have a reputation that you feel you can't get rid of. Maybe you feel disqualified. Or maybe you just lost hope in yourself. If we look at the story of Paul before he wrote most of the New Testament, he was Saul of Tarsus, a modern-day Gangster to the early church. Not only was he present when Stephen, the first Christian martyr was killed, but he also gave the green light to the murder. (Acts 7:57–8:1)

Luke explains that Saul made it his business to destroy the church. He made it personal, going door to door in Jerusalem, looking for people who followed Jesus to throw them in prison or worst murdered them. (Acts 8:3) After putting these people in prison, he planned to hunt down the Christians he received by letters. (Acts 22:4–5) While he was on his way, he had an encounter that changed his life and the world forever, making the rest history.

Paul began to change each day and grow but not grow in the same mindset but in a new one. Paul's letter to Timothy said, "Here is a trustworthy saying that deserves full acceptance: Christ Jesus came into the world to save sinners—of whom I am the worst. But for that very reason I was shown mercy so that in me, the worst of sinners, Christ Jesus might display his immense patience as an example for those who would believe in him and receive eternal life."

(1 Tim. 1:15–16 NIV)

Growth happens in a leap of faith.

Living the life you want often means you have to make some significant changes in every part of your life, whether if it's your career, relationships, or where you are living. Change can sound like a good idea in theory, but, in practice, it's not always so clear and pretty. This is where we all have struggles. We tend to believe that change is challenging if we can actually shift our life in the direction we want to go. Or, if you succeed, it's hard to know whether that change will be what you really want. Ultimately, if you really want to change your life, you must have the risk of taking a leap of faith. The leap of faith begins with the conviction that you don't want to go down the path that your current life has been taking you any longer, that your life just isn't working for you any longer. Faith is a power we all possessed. You can have a bag full of faith or a simple mustard seed of faith. A mustard seed faith is just as powerful as a bag full of faith. The power to move mountains isn't because of our own strength but on who we draw our strength from. Nothing becomes impossible and with God, each risk is doable.

"He replied, "Because you have so little faith. Truly I tell you, if you have faith as small as a mustard seed, you can say to this mountain, 'Move from here to there,' and it will move. Nothing will be impossible for you."""
Matthew 17:20 NIV

The leap of faith is faith that you can change your life. It involves having a belief in Jesus and a fundamental trust in the vision of who you are, what you are going to be, and where you want to be in the future. Your leap involves believing that good things will happen when you choose to take a risk and change your life. Growing pains are healthy for your future, grab hold of your faith and continue to press through.

Reflect on who you are

Inner self-reflection is something that many people like to avoid because they are worried about what they could find, so we avoid it at all costs. Many times, in life, I kept telling myself I was someone I was not. This blocked my growth in areas that needed to grow. But we need to know who you are deep inside. There is a part of us that no other person knows, except for you and God. To know who you are and who you want to show the world, you have to look inside yourself and ask, "who am I?"

Don't worry what the world may say who you are, what society may say who you are, what your coworkers may say who you are, even your family; pay no attention to who they say you are. If God said you are unique, you have value, your life has a purpose, then start treating your life with value and purpose and someone who isn't ordinary but someone extraordinary. Grow in who God says you are and not what people say you are. If you want to be a person of influence, reflect on how you can change your life for others.

Grow in who God says you are and not what people say you are

Your age does not disqualify you

I love the conversations I hear on risk taking. It's ironic to me when I hear people say risk taking are only found at a young age as if there is a cut off to taking risks. You are never too old or too young reinvent yourself. Or to try something new. There is no age limit. The possibilities are endless so do not let people tell you otherwise. The world we are living in right now has evolved into a place where anything is possible at any age, so take your time. You owe it to no one else but yourself to truly be happy. At 8 years old, a child made 26 million in 2019 on YouTube, mostly by reviewing toys. Let's allow that to sink in for a second. Moving forward to a remarkable man who didn't find success until his 60s. This man's name was Harland Sanders, the founder of Kentucky Fried Chicken. Sanders was an entrepreneur at an early age who didn't become a professional chef until he was 40 years old. He didn't stop there, after going from restaurant to restaurant and being persistent, Sanders didn't franchise Kentucky Fried Chicken until he was 62 years old. He still wasn't done; he didn't become the icon we all know and grew up on until after he sold his company at the age of 75. Fear will tell you at your age you are unable to restart or begin new. As long as you still have a heartbeat then the future is still bright, and the risk is still worth taking. We see in the bible many stories of many different people being used, all at different ages such as Abraham being used at the age of 100 to parent Isaac and David being anointed around the age of 15. At any age we are still growing and learning. You can succeed at any age as long as you take the risk and learn to be teachable.

You are never too old or too young to reinvent yourself

New growth chases success

Kobe Bryant once said, "Once you know what failure feels like, determination chases success." I want to be the best version of myself. And because of that, I know I will make mistakes, but I will not let my mistakes be my end result. Each risk, each moment of growth, is making me a better person for my future. My past mistakes, tears, and moments of distress are just growing pains that too shall pass. A new day is ahead of me. I will allow growth to define me.

I will not let my mistakes be my end result

Chapter 9

Make the Risk Personal

‘Setbacks motivate me." — Lindsey Vonn, Alpine Ski Racer.

I think it's safe to say we pick and choose what's important to us. When something matters to you, you treat it differently. The value of it becomes different from everything else. The way I treat my Yeezy's compare to how I treat a pair of vans are entirely different. It's because I find value in my Yeezy's. It goes the same with the dreams I have in life. I have to prioritize what's more important. What am I able to go without and what am I not able to give up? We all have dreams we want to accomplish, and to do so, we first have to mentally be serious about it. Meaning we must be mentally prepared that it won't be easy, and it will cost you to sacrifice a lot of comfort in your life. I want to win in life.

I want to win as a father, as a husband, as a Pastor, and as a man in general. I want to win in every area. When I fall short in these areas, how I comeback sets my future self to not make the same mistake. I want to encourage you to carry the same mindset. In life and for your future. Career-wise and finically. Even if you don't plan on starting your own business and if you want to climb the corporate ladder, how do you react towards a setback or a loss? Do you take it personally? Make it personal to a point you are willing to try again. Most people fail in life because they give up after the first try.

The fear within…

All of us have fears that reside deep within our hearts. There is a fear of failure, rejection, criticism, embarrassment, and even fear of making mistakes. It becomes more challenging, especially when it's personal. There will always be fear, even stepping out in faith. The goal is to push through and always remember. If it goes as plan or if it does not, you took a risk you haven't done before. All of these fears get in our way and prevent us from taking risks, but you didn't allow it. We believe we are fine where we are and don't need to move further, so we get stuck.

This is a toxic trait, and we have to move past it. The moment we allow other people to dictate our choices and decisions, we are putting our lives and fate in someone else's hands. 9 times out of 10, this will not end well for us. Therefore, we need to get out of this mindset and focus on what will allow us to take the risk.

Irrational needs

We have these needs inside of us, and while some of them are valid and deserve to be paid attention to, some are just irrational, and we need to identify them. For instance, our need for approval, play it safe, and the need to avoid feeling guilty can create problems. For some of us, there is a need to make excuses that are holding us back from living the life we desire. We have to understand that all of this is in our heads. These barriers have been put there by our own selves. It is a way to protect ourselves from the aftermath, which might not work in our favor.

But we need to know that we do not have to play it safe all the time. We don't need to avoid guilt as it can help us to make better decisions in the future. But we do need to balance out the right kinds of risks at the right time. If you continue to shy away from risks, you will regret it in the long run. No one became someone without ever taking the risk. History is full of such examples.

No one became someone without ever taking the risk

Irrational habits

Habits are a part of us. In fact, sometimes, they are so deeply engraved into our minds that we don't realize the power that they have. Yes, they can dominate us and our actions if we don't watch it. When you take risks, there are some habits that you will need to steer clear from so that you can take risks that are going to improve life.

Relying on others

Most of us have this habit. We have a tendency to rely on other people to solve our problems and take responsibility from our hands. It is easy to just sit back and let someone else solve our problems for us. Have you ever been in a group project in school and one person in the group did absolutely nothing but still got an A from the work of everyone else in the group? Yes, I'm also talking about those people. This also means that someone else is taking the risk on our behalf. So if things turn out in our favor, we all are good. If they don't, well…we can always blame someone else for it. This is wrong. Never give the power to transform your life to someone else. Yes, it is nice to hide behind someone else when things go wrong, but it will not help us achieve anything. Least of all our goals.

Overthinking and its consequences

I think people tend to overthink. A lot, I'm still one of them. Nothing good really comes from overthinking and this is really just another form of procrastination. You will only be thinking about the details without doing anything productive. It can lead to hesitation and failure of action on your part. This means there will be less risk-taking behavior.

Denial

Denial works well for people. In fact, I sometimes envy those people. It's easy to act like a problem is not really there. Sometimes we can be like the cartoon dog's meme at the table surrounded by fire and saying everything is fine. How can people just shut their eyes to reality? Denying that problems exist or showing no willingness to take any responsibility for the problems will prevent you from taking risks. To overcome these problems, you need to take risks, and here's the catch. To take risks, you have to first accept that you have the problem. Imagine that your life is a giant puzzle. You need to put the puzzle together and once you do, you start to get some kind of a picture. If you are willing to take responsibility for it, you will reap your actions' benefits. Just give it a try, you will really appreciate the outcome.

Lacking something…

Perhaps you are not taking risks because you do not believe in yourself. You feel you do not have the self-confidence or belief in your abilities. It may also come down to your inability to change. You resist change, for whatever reasons, and you are unwilling to move past that. Identify within yourself what exactly holds you back and then move forward.

For instance, if you lack confidence, you can efficiently work on that by boosting your confidence level. This will help you develop the courage you need to make the right decisions about yourself. Something that can definitely help you in life. Perhaps you are one of those that do not want to change, find reasons to change. This will motivate you to take risks and take chances. Ask yourself why you want to make changes in your life, why it is so important and what your life would look like if you made these changes.

The risk assessment guide:

The following are just some of the things you can do to assess risk before taking it:

Identifying your goals

One of the first things you can do is think about the goals you have in mind. Once you are clear on that, the next thing to do is understand the outcomes and the consequences of these outcomes in your life. Like in the previous chapter, we need to ask ourselves the outcome that you will have in your life and what you could potentially lose from this. When you take risks, you will often find that you lose nothing. By learning from the loss, you actually didn't lose. You may also find that you are at a more significant loss for not having taken the risk at all.

The second thing that you can do is to identify the obstacles that stand in your way. Look at what you will need to do to remove those obstacles. Ask yourself what you are uncertain about, the worst thing that could happen, and if the risk is worth the reward you are about to take. Hopefully, these questions will give you a more precise answer.

Take lessons from the past.

Before you hurry and take on new risks, make sure that the past lessons are there for you. Bring them forward to make sure that you don't make the same mistakes twice. You should ask yourself if you have done this before, if others have fared from taking this path, and some of the mistakes you made earlier. If you feel that you are entering into entirely new territory, perhaps draw a parallel from the past lessons to see how you can avoid the same mistakes. Remember, we learn more from past mistakes and your own experiences than from someone telling you what to do.

Developing plans

You have to create an action plan and a timeframe to know the results you are expecting. You need to define your timings, resources, and knowledge so that you can achieve what you are setting out to achieve. Ask yourself the best time to take the risk, how you will handle the outcome, and what you can do to ensure that this results in success. The answer will come to you.

Evaluating the outcome

Once you have done everything necessary, you need to evaluate the outcomes and feelings. Even if things did not go according to plan, you could still use this evaluation time to make plans for your future. You have to remember that the risks will not always pan out the way we want them to. There are times when you will be successful, and this is the time that you want to hold on to. There are also times when you will not be as successful in your effort, but instead of stepping away from the path altogether, you need to make peace with it, so it does not interfere with your future actions. Ask yourself what you have learned from this experience and how you can carry it forward in the future. The answer will come!

By learning from the loss, you actually didn't lose

Chapter 10

Final Thoughts

"Everybody has an addiction, mine happens to be success."

– Drake

I've spent a lot of time recently with business owners. Different business owners who own barbershops, a nutrition company, real estate, handyman services, and dispensary owners to coffee shop owners. The list goes on. I've noticed from every business owner I sat down with that they all share the same risk they all took to get where they are today and the risk they will continue to take to keep their business thriving. I'm learning it's not just one risk you take, and then it's over. The first risk is the beginning of many more to come. Taking a risk is the first step to accomplishing what's on your heart. Every person who is looking for greatness needs to be able to take risks to thrive for greatness. Greatness comes not as a gift but from hard work and dedication. Enduring the journey from good to great in the job position you are in or any title you may have on yourself. Be the best at it and continue to learn and grow.

Taking a risk is the first step to accomplishing what's on your heart.

Chase success

When you make a choice and say, "I am going to give it my all, I am going to be this" then you should not be surprised when you are that. Despite how hard it is, hard work is needed. Dedication is mandatory. A friend of mine once told me, "heavy is the crown." He was explaining to me that my time and energy have to be focused on succeeding for the day. Nothing else should matter until your responsibility is completed. Nobody who lives a normal life succeeds because they get distracted easily. Social media, texting, Netflix. We live in a generation full of distractions. We need to live a life beyond normal. If we can be self-discipline, imagine all that you can accomplish.

"If you are not willing to risk the unusual, you will have to settle for the ordinary."

– Jim Rohn

We have to understand something. The fears that we have are irrational, for the most part. We cannot defeat them if we only think about what can go wrong. Instead, we have to think about what will happen if things go right. This will make you feel more motivated, and you will want to achieve that goal. In turn, you will also take the first step needed to defeat the challenge. This is only possible if you take the risk. Forget about the fear of failing. Forget about falling on your feet. Just take the risk; I promise that it is going to be worth it. Also, once you do take that first risk, you will feel so much lighter. It is as if the entire boulder has been lifted off your shoulder.

There is no going back to the place you came from. Even the fear would have left you…to some extent. Next time, you will not be hesitant and take the first step without overthinking what will happen. Now, in all likelihood, you will be able to look at your challenge in the face and know that you have what it takes to overpower it.

Pursuing your dreams

The dream is your vision, goal, and desire. You can label it any way you want. These are things that most of us have, and we need them. We touched on chapter two regarding dreams. There is no concept of success without dreams. The sad part is that we have forgotten all about them.

Too often, we forget what life all is about. Did you know that the secret of living is giving? If you were to follow your dreams, then you will have something to hold on to. You can also share it easily with other people, your dreams are an inspiration and can be a candle of light to the ones around you. For some people, it might actually be the hope that they need to hold on to. The power of impact your dream can have if you unlock it.

When we chase our dreams and not daydream, we develop and strengthen our courage. Courage is our fuel to achieve tremendous success in life. We have to chase our dreams and achieve the level of courage that will ensure we are unstoppable.

"If you can dream it, you can do it."

—Walt Disney.

Courage is our fuel to achieve tremendous success in life.

Additionally, when you chase your dreams, you come to appreciate the word failure. As unlikely as that sounds, it is very accurate. Your perception changes and you understand that failure is integral to success. So we don't look at failure as failure. It highlighted the path you are going to take, which is enough for many people. As Kobe Bryant said, failure doesn't exist. Because it showed us a different way of doing things. It became a lesson and not the end of the stop. So chase your dream. Chase your dream as much as you can and never be afraid to dream big. I have noticed that some people are just so scared of thinking beyond the boundaries they have set in their heads. They don't realize what they are doing. The only reason that they are following a particular path is that it is the easiest. Easy never really got anyone anywhere. You have to be true to yourself and follow your dreams. You need to know that you are not doing anyone any favors, least yourself by living a lie.

Chase your dream as much as you can and never be afraid to dream big

The comfort zone

Chapter six, we discussed the danger of the comfort zone. The ability to take risks by stepping outside of the comfort zone is the primary way to grow. But the problem we continue to face is that we really don't want to leave the comfort zone behind. We are unwilling to even take the first step. I took the time to talk to unsuccessful people. Come to find out they aren't hard to find. I've realized they didn't become unsuccessful because of bad business decisions or taking a finical hit but from the very fact of not leaving the comfort zone.

Fear resides in the comfort zone. We are afraid to step outside into the unknown. I encourage you to break the chains that bond you to fear. Once you let go and step out of fear you are able to love life a little more which would allow you to take more risks with more confidence.

The following are just some of the ways that you can step outside of your comfort zone:

Becoming aware

Think of all the things that you believe are worth doing. Think about them and list them down. Then ask yourself why you are so afraid of them. Perhaps it is because you feel there is potential for disappointment or failure. Dig deep into yourself and find the answer. It is there, just trust your gut.

Hang out with risk-takers

You will learn a lot from them. If you want to become better at something or loosen up in general, you have to hang out with people who like to test their boundaries. Their effect will start to rub off on you, and before you know it, you will be one of those who are taking risks. Never be afraid to ask questions. This is very important. I've learned this a little too late in life, but it's never too late to ask questions. Study what made risk-takers, risk-takers.

"As iron sharpens iron, so a friend sharpens a friend."
Proverbs 27:17 NLT

Honesty

You have to be honest with yourself. This is key. This is one of the most trusted ways to become successful. Do not make excuses for the shortcomings. Be honest with where you have failed and know that you can only overcome it if you know what lies inside you.

"Honesty prospers in every condition of life."
- Friedrich Schiller

Look at the benefits

Look at the benefits. Understand how things will work to your advantage. For instance, if you start to engage in public speaking, your opinions will be heard worldwide. You will also become more confident, and this will also help you in your job interviews. The benefits to anything are many if we just choose to see it. The benefits of taking risk is that it makes you a better person.

Failure

Failure is going to occur, regardless of what we do. It's the risk we talked about in chapter three. We can put in the best efforts and think we have nailed it, but the outcome is that we have failed. I want you to imagine this. Your dream job has called, and they are going to interview you. You know what has to be done. This is your dream job, and you have been preparing for it for a long time. You know the kind of questions they will ask, and you know how to answer them. The answers are at your fingertips. The day arrives, and you dress up and head towards the office. You are a bit nervous but otherwise confident. You know you are going to ace this.

You step into the interview room and answer all the questions correctly. You know you have done an excellent job, I mean come on, it's you. Your interview was so smooth, they should have made the offer to you there and then. You go home and relax. You are expected to have your dream job now. You wait, but no call comes. You refresh your email, waiting for the day it will come. You know it's coming but nothing comes, and you start getting scared. The doubt begins, and then that day comes, you get the email of rejection.

You wonder what happened to you and where you went wrong. The self-doubt eats you up. And you are ready to quit life. This happened to a close friend of mine but let me tell you what I told him. This is not the end. There is a future for you and a calling on your life only you can answer. God will open the right door for you. There is so much more to life. If you go and start your very first company and spent all your money on investments to launch only to crash and close down, we keep pushing forward. There are new doors ready to be opened only by you. You have the key to unlock your potential, and the key is in your risk.

"The Lord says: You know if a man falls down, he gets up again. And if a man goes the wrong way, he turns around and comes back." (Jerimiah 8:4)

Take a risk knowing God is in control. You have what it takes to go and make a difference in your life. You have the potential in you. fulfill your vision, live the life you were called to live and not the life you have settled with.

Conclusion

"When writing the story of your life, don't let anyone else hold the pen." -Drake

Drake is arguably one of the best artists in music today. I love my conversations I have with other people on this topic. So, it's safe to say I am a fan. Since his first album, Drake continued to grow as an artist and dominate charts along the way. His fifth album, “Scorpion” made him the first artist to top one billion streams in one week. Come on! Started from the bottom, now we here. This type of success is off of the motivation and passion he has for what he does. It doesn’t just stop in music, it continued in business and in life. He has said on record many times how he is addicted to success. Your passion for more will have you addicted. It will have you thinking of it day and night. Nothing else will matter just as Kobe Bryant was towards basketball. You are addicted to what’s important to you. What is consuming your time? Are you growing as an individual? Are you developing a better future or are you perfecting your sleep?

“So I saw that there is nothing better for people than to be happy in their work. That is our lot in life. And no one can bring us back to see what happens after we die.” Ecclesiastes 3:22 NLT

The calling on your life is remarkable because God gave each and every one of you a calling and purpose. Your life has meaning, your life has value. See yourself the way God sees you, worthy of his love. Take a risk and go after what God has placed on your heart. The desires deep within was not meant to be hidden. Uncover your talent and let it blossom. Acknowledge failure as a steppingstone to keep going. I pray this book is a key to unlock the best version of you.

"For God's gifts and his call can never be withdrawn."
Romans 11:29 NLT

I encourage you to keep exploring how you can tap into a better you through work, business, family, or an unborn idea. Life has a funny way of bringing us back to our calling despite our attempts to ignore it. Nothing will come easy and seeing it through can be even harder, but God often presents opportunities to absorb our passion. Trust yourself. Believing in yourself can be incredibly easy when you know who has your back. Know that God has your best interests at heart and that he will make every attempt to see your dreams come to fruition as long as you keep pursuing. It may feel scary. If you're uncertain, if you want to give up, give it one more day. New days are new beginnings. You are worth every ounce of your effort. There are people all around who will benefit from you taking a risk and following your heart. Don't abandon your gift. Take the risk.